SUPER ENGINEER

BUILD YOUR OWN AIRCRAFT

Thanks to the creative team:

Senior Editor: Alice Peebles
Fact checking: Tom Jackson
Design: Perfect Bound Ltd

First published in Great Britain in 2018
by Hungry Tomato Ltd
PO Box 181
Edenbridge
Kent, TN8 9DP

A CIP catalogue record for this book is
available from the British Library.

ISBN 978-1-912108-61-9

Printed and bound in China

Discover more at
www.hungrytomato.com

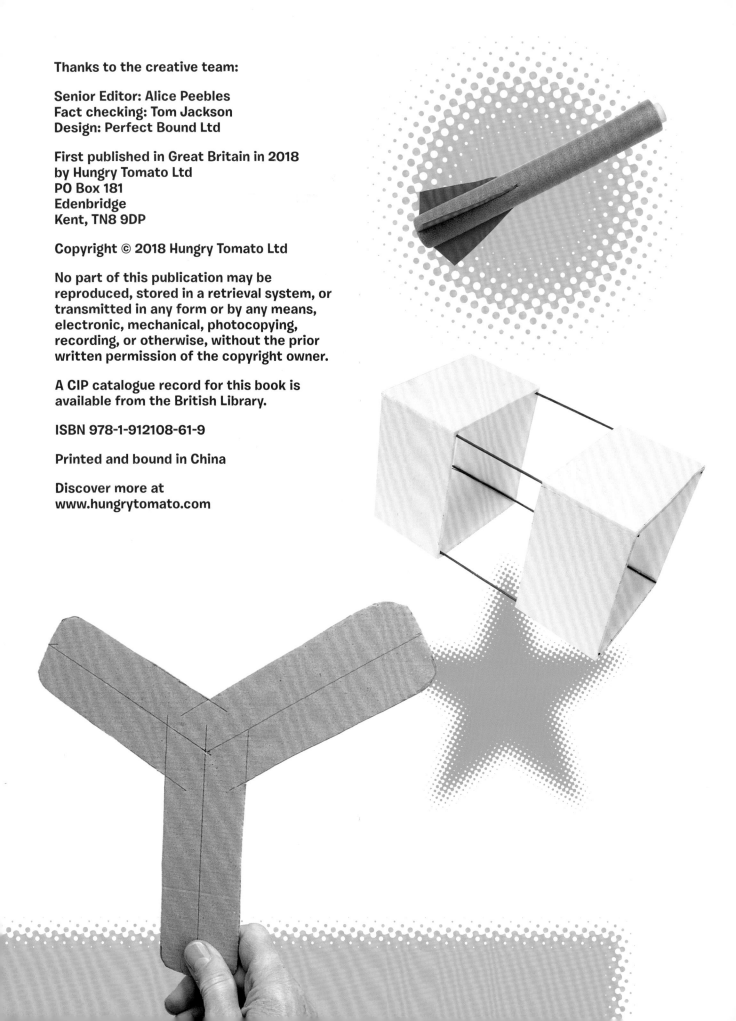

SUPER ENGINEER

BUILD YOUR OWN AIRCRAFT

BY **ROB IVES**

HUNGRY
TOMATO™

SAFETY FIRST

Take care and use good sense when making these fun model aircraft – they are all quite straightforward, but you will need to cut materials, drill holes etc, for which it's handy to have an adult assistant (see below).

Every project includes a list of everything you will need to do it. Most will be stuff you can find around the house, or is readily available and inexpensive to buy online or from a local hardware or general-purpose store.

We have also included 'How It Works' for each model, to explain in simple terms the engineering or scientific principles that make it work. And for some there is a 'Real-world Engineering' snippet that applies these principles to actual machines.

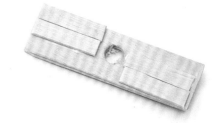

Watch out for this sign accompanying some model instructions. You may need help from an adult with completing these tasks.

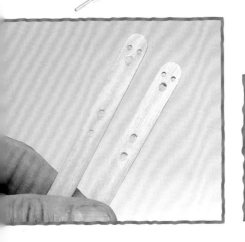

DISCLAIMER

The author, publisher and bookseller cannot take responsibility for your safety. When you make and try out the projects, you do so at your own risk. Look out for the safety warning symbol (above) given throughout the book and call on adult assistance when you are cutting materials or testing out the models.

CONTENTS

(Words in **bold** are explained here)

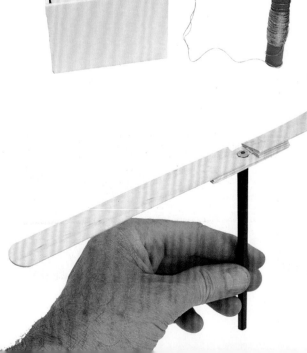

AIRCRAFT

Isn't it amazing how a big, heavy object can get up in the air and stay there... Of course, it took a while for inventors to get that to happen, with lots of experimenting along the way. Some of them started by making bird-like wings and flapping them – and they're still perfecting the design!

Now you can be your own inventor with these eight cool models based on all kinds of aircraft from those early days onwards. Even though they're obviously small and very light, they still won't stay up without the right engineering. None of them has engine power, so find out how they do it!

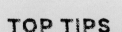

Take your box kite outdoors and see just how high this high flyer can reach, launch a helicopter or watch your glider go – and keep on going! The airship might not make a transatlantic flight, as the most powerful ones did, but it may go *much* further than you expect, and it can certainly hover!

So get your tools and materials together, start building and see how these craft float and fly like the birds – the best fliers of all...

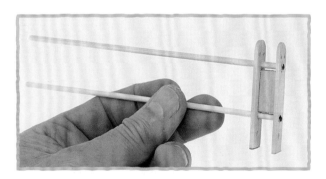

TOP TIPS

- Before you start on any of the models, read the step-by-steps all the way through to get an idea of what you're aiming for. The pictures show what the steps tell you to do.

- Some projects need pencils to be cut into sections. Do ask for help with this and use a cutting mat, or similar surface to cut on. An efficient way to do it is to cut each face of the pencil in turn with a craft knife, then snap it apart. Tidy up any unevenness with the knife.

TOOL KIT
- Pencil
- Ruler (long and standard)
- Craft knife
- Pair of compasses
- Marker pen
- Gaffer tape
- Double-sided tape
- String
- Small clamps or clothes pegs
- Screwdriver
- Long-nose pliers
- Hot glue gun
- Craft drill
- Wire cutters
- PVA glue
- Drawing pin
- Super glue
- Kitchen scissors
- Cutting mat

PVA

SUPER GLUE

GLIDING ALONG

No engine noise and brilliant flying – that's what's great about gliders. Let those air currents do the work!

TOOLS:
- String
- Scissors
- Marker pen
- Long ruler
- Craft knife
- Hot glue gun

YOU WILL NEED:

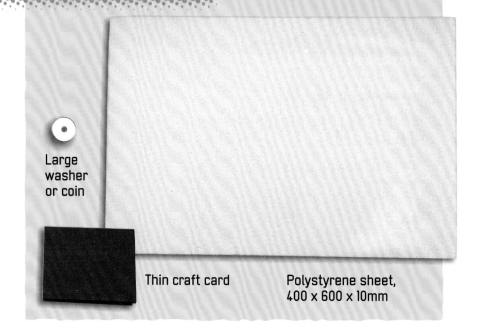

Large washer or coin

Thin craft card

Polystyrene sheet, 400 x 600 x 10mm

1 Starting from one corner of the polystyrene sheet, mark out a quarter circle using the string looped around the pen as shown. (The width of the sheet is the radius of the circle.)

2 Mark off about 360mm centrally along the edge of the quarter cirle, to get an arc. Mark a central tail section, 120mm wide.

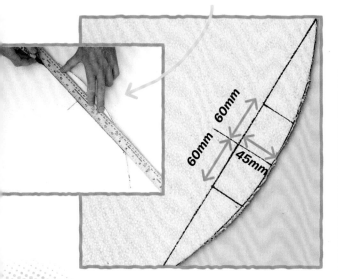

60mm
60mm
60mm
45mm

Tail
Fin
Fin

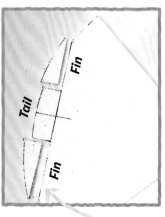

3 Cut off the two pieces next to the tail to use as tail fins. Use the construction guides opposite to cut out two flaps and two rudders from thin card. Check that they will fit on as shown in step 5.

4 Use a hot glue gun to glue the polystyrene fins to the tail.

Glue a large washer or coin to the nose of the glider.

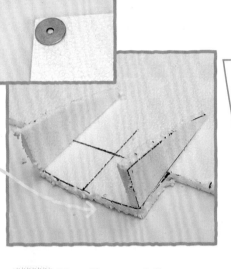

Flap construction guide

Rudder construction guide

5 Glue the card flaps to the glider body and the rudders to the tail fins as shown.

Hold the glider at head height and let it fall forward from your hand – there's no need to throw it.

WHEEEE!

You'll need plenty of space – it will fly for 30 metres!

HOW IT WORKS

The glider is made from polystyrene, a very **low-density** material. Its large surface area means that there is a lot of **air resistance** pushing upwards to keep it airborne. But because it is very thin, it easily cuts through the air. The small weight on the front helps to keep the glider moving forwards.

REAL-WORLD ENGINEERING

A glider has to fly fast enough for its wings to produce the **lift** to keep it aloft. It can gain speed by aiming slightly downwards. It also uses **thermals**, columns of warm air rising from the ground, to counteract its descending glide and stay in the air.

BOO-OO-OO-MERANG

The boomerang is an iconic hunting weapon used with great skill by Australian aboriginals. It's depicted in some of the world's oldest rock art.

TOOLS:
- Ruler
- String
- Cutting mat
- Drawing pin
- Pencil
- Craft knife

YOU WILL NEED:

A large piece of corrugated card, about 350mm wide

1 Cut a piece of string just less than half the width of your card. Tie a loop in both ends. Lay the card on the cutting mat, and press the drawing pin into the centre, catching one loop on your string. With the pencil inside the other loop, draw a large circle by keeping the string taut.

2 Draw a line from the centre to the edge of the circle.

3 Move the drawing pin and loop to where these lines meet. Use the pencil and same length of string to mark off a small arc on the edge of the circle.

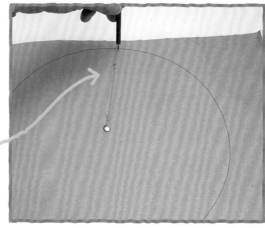

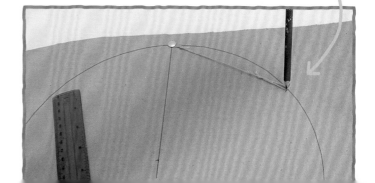

4 Repeat to mark off another arc, and continue to do this all the way round the circle.

5 Draw two more lines from the centre to the outside of the circle as shown.

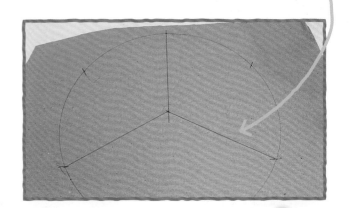

6 Line your ruler up against each of these three lines and draw parallel lines a ruler's width away on either side.

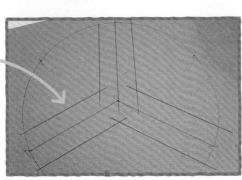

7 Carefully cut out the shape with a craft knife. Cut rounded corners and curve the leading edges over by 15mm.

Rounded corners

Bend these edges down

Initial flight path

Boomerang gradually turns in a curved flight path

Rotation

HOW IT WORKS

The long arms of the boomerang give it a **gyroscope** effect, so that it keeps spinning after it is thrown. The curved blades work like a propeller, pushing the boomerang continuously to one side and curving its flight. This is why it eventually returns to the thrower.

Throw the boomerang with a flick of the wrist...

SWISSHH!

...be ready for it to come back!

AIRY AIRSHIP

Airships are lighter-than-air aircraft. They were the first aircraft capable of controlled, powered flight.

YOU WILL NEED:

Sheet of plain paper

Thin elastic band

Button thread

5mm plastic bead

Helium-filled foil balloon

Wooden skewer, 3mm thick

Two small paper clips

Coffee stirring stick

... and you may need modelling clay

TOOLS:

- Wire cutters
- Long-nose pliers
- Craft knife
- Craft drill
- PVA glue
- Ruler
- Pencil
- Scissors
- Double-sided tape

1 Cut a paper clip in half with wire cutters and shape each half as shown with pliers.

2 Cut a 170mm length of wooden skewer with a craft knife. Drill a 2mm hole 20mm from each end with a craft drill.

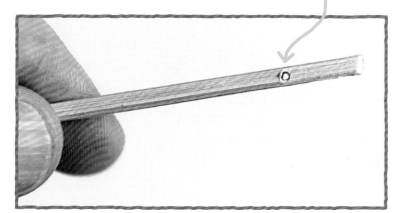

12

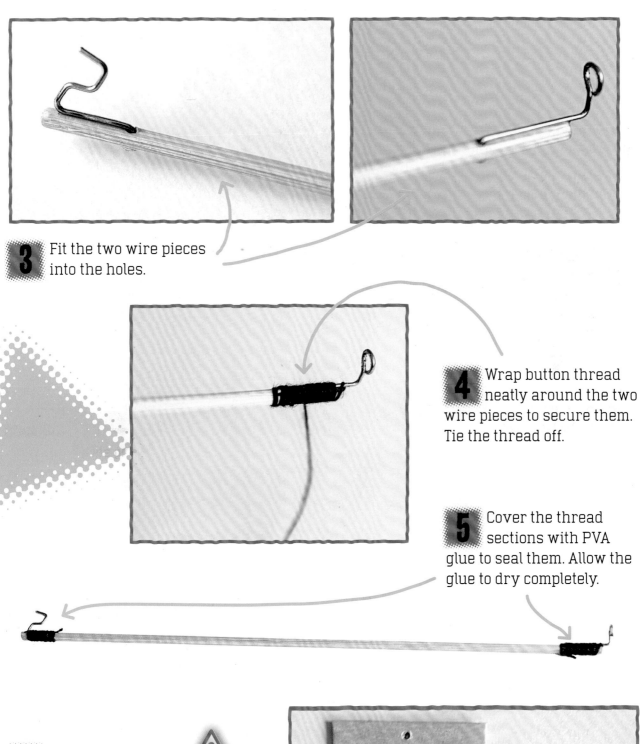

3 Fit the two wire pieces into the holes.

4 Wrap button thread neatly around the two wire pieces to secure them. Tie the thread off.

5 Cover the thread sections with PVA glue to seal them. Allow the glue to dry completely.

6 Cut a second paper clip in half and make a loop at the end.
Cut a 20mm length from the coffee stirring stick and drill a 2mm hole in the middle.

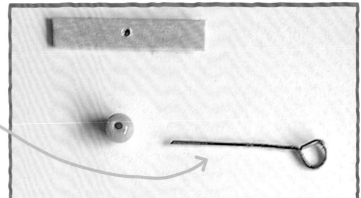

7 Thread the wire through the fixed loop on the skewer, then the bead and the hole in the coffee stirrer.

8 Shape the end of the wire as shown and glue it to the stirrer with PVA glue. This completes the centre of the propeller.

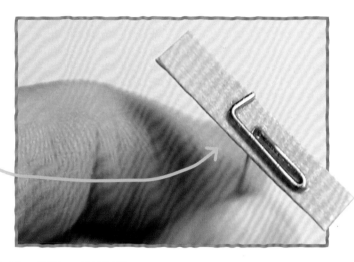

9 Stretch a thin elastic band between the hook on the propeller centre and the other end of the skewer.

10 Use the template as a guide to draw and cut out two propeller blades from paper to the measurements given. Glue them to the coffee stirrer.
Bend over one edge on each by 3mm as shown.

20mm

55mm

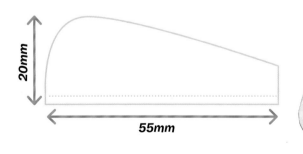

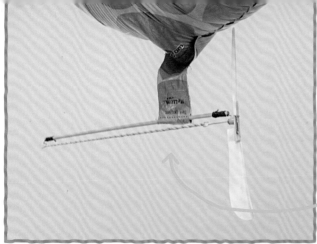

11 Attach the balloon to the skewer with double-sided tape. The **airship** should hang in the air without moving up or down. If not, find the point where the skewer is balanced and add a blob of modelling clay.

Wind up the prop and release, so your airship will **fly!**

SSSHHH!

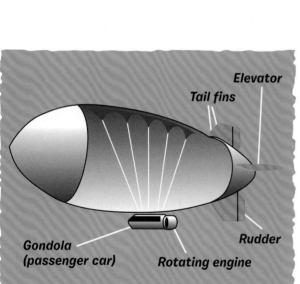

Elevator
Tail fins
Gondola (passenger car)
Rotating engine
Rudder

HOW IT WORKS

The airship floats in air just like a submarine floats in water. The balloon is filled with helium, a very low-density gas. The balloon and propeller **displace** exactly the same weight of air as their combined weight, so the airship hangs in the air. The propeller, turned by the elastic band unwinding, pushes air backwards, moving the airship forwards.

REAL-WORLD ENGINEERING

Early airships were huge envelopes filled with a lifting gas (hydrogen or helium) that was less dense than the air. They were powered by gas or petrol engines. Rigid airships were manufactured by the German Zeppelin factory, after whom they were named. From 1928, the enormous airship, 127 *Graf Zeppelin* ran the world's first (and very successful) passenger flight service across the Atlantic.

FLOATING 'CHUTE

The word 'parachute' says it all: para (against), chute (fall). A party tablecloth makes a colourful one!

TOOLS:
- Long ruler
- Scissors
- Marker pen

YOU WILL NEED:

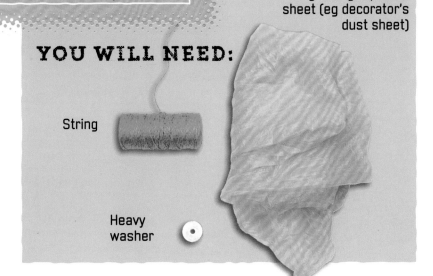

Lightweight plastic sheet (eg decorator's dust sheet)

String

Heavy washer

---

1 Cut a 500mm square piece of plastic sheet. Fold it in half.

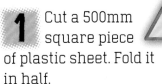

2 Fold in one side from the centre to the measurement shown.

250mm

106mm

3 Repeat on the other side so the edges line up.

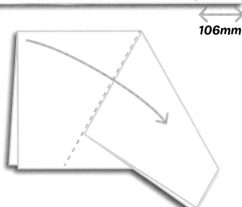

4 Cut straight across, so you get a whole, folded triangle.

5 Before you unfold the triangle, mark the six lower corners all round so you can find them easily.

6 Cut 20mm off the apex of the triangle (a hole in the centre stablizes the parachute's flight). Unfold the triangle to reveal a large hexagon.

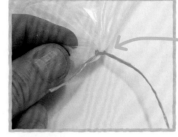

7 Cut six lengths of string, 500mm long. Tie a piece of string to each corner of the 'chute.

8 Gather the strings together so that the corner knots are at even height.

9 Tie a heavy washer to the other ends of the string.

9 Gather the parachute from the centre again, then fold it in two a couple of times and wrap the string round it.

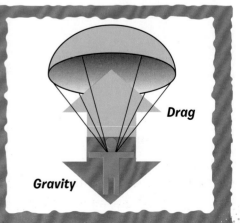

Go outside, throw it as high as you can and watch it drift slowly back to Earth!

HOW IT WORKS

The large surface area of the parachute catches the air as it falls and provides lots of **drag**. This slows down the payload (whatever it's carrying) to a safe speed. A parachute can be used for dropping goods in remote locations, saving lives and even for delivering a lander to a planet's surface! A falling person without a parachute will reach around 190 km/h (120 mph), called the **terminal velocity**. A parachute reduces this speed to a much safer 25–30 km/h (15–20 mph).

Drag

Gravity

WHIRLING HELICOPTER

Choppers require special pilot skills. So start by trying out this mini heli. No licence required.

TOOLS:
- Ruler
- Kitchen scissors
- PVA glue
- Small clamps or clothes pegs
- 7mm craft drill
- Craft knife

YOU WILL NEED:

Pencil

Coffee stirring sticks

Four wide lolly sticks

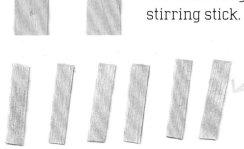

1 Cut two 60mm lengths of lolly stick with scissors. Cut six 20mm lengths of coffee stirring stick.

2 Glue the lolly sticks together with PVA glue. Hold them with small clamps or clothes pegs while the glue dries.

3 Drill a pencil-width hole in the middle of the lolly sticks with a craft drill.

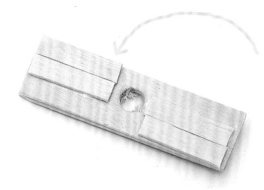

4 Glue four of the coffee stick pieces in place as shown.

5 Glue the remaining two on the outside pieces to make a double layer.

6 Apply a generous layer of PVA glue, covering stirrers and stick as shown.

7 Cut one curved end from two lolly sticks. Clamp the straight end of the stick in place as shown. Repeat on the other side. ⚠️

8 Cut the point off the pencil with a craft knife and discard. Fit the pencil into the hole. ⚠️

Spin it between the palms of your hands in one direction...

FWHIP!

...and let it **fly!**

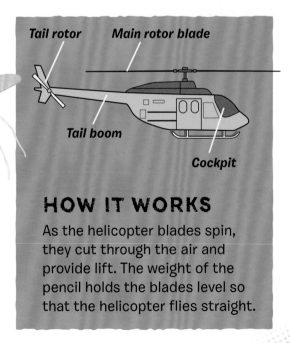

Tail rotor *Main rotor blade*

Tail boom

Cockpit

HOW IT WORKS

As the helicopter blades spin, they cut through the air and provide lift. The weight of the pencil holds the blades level so that the helicopter flies straight.

HIGH FLYER

Box kites hold the record for the highest flight, at over 16,000ft (4,800m)! They were used in World War II to hold radio aerials aloft and to tow life rafts.

TOOLS:
- Long ruler
- Craft knife
- Hot glue gun
- Skewer or pencil

Four 600mm garden canes (the thinnest available)

150mm length of poster tube

Two polystyrene sheets, 600 x 400 x 10mm

Nylon garden string

Split ring

1 Use a craft knife to cut eight equal polystyrene pieces, 300 x 200mm.

2 Use the hot glue gun to glue four pieces together along their narrower edges.

3 Repeat to make an exact match for the kite's other half.

4 Use the hot glue gun to glue the garden canes inside the box corners as shown.

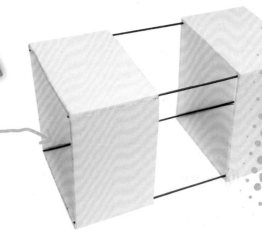

POKE

5 Cut a 700mm length of string. Make holes in a top corner of the kite with a skewer or pencil point. Push one end of the string in and around the cane and tie it on. Add a split ring to the rest of the string, just above the midpoint, with a crow's foot knot (see page 30). Tie the string to the cane above the lower section.

You only need a light wind to get your kite to fly!

6 Tie the end of a 30m length of string round the poster tube. Wrap it round the tube, then tie the other end to the split ring with a crow's foot hitch knot (see page 30).

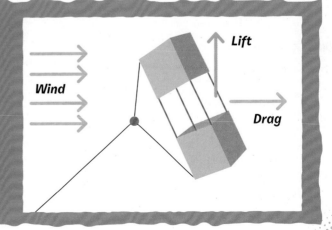

HOW IT WORKS

The box kite design is very stable and works well even in low winds. The forces at work on it are the same as for any other aircraft: lift, weight and drag. Lift is the force that gets the kite into the air. When wind moves around the box structure, there is more pressure up from the bottom than down from the top, so up it goes. The kite is kept airborne by wind flowing through it.

Lift

Wind

Drag

ORNITHOPTER

This early flying machine was named after the Greek *ornithos* for bird, and *pteron*, wing. They were so-called because people strapped on wings and tried to fly like birds.

TOOLS:
- Craft drill
- Craft knife
- Ruler
- PVA glue
- Long-nose pliers
- Pair of compasses
- Scissors
- Super glue
- Double-sided tape

YOU WILL NEED:

Heavy elastic band

Corrugated cardboard offcut

Heavy plastic shopping bag

Three 5mm plastic beads

Three lolly sticks

Four 250mm wooden skewers, 3mm thick

Coffee stirring sticks

Button thread

Small paper clips

Eraser

2mm *for the end holes*

3mm *for the inner holes*

2mm

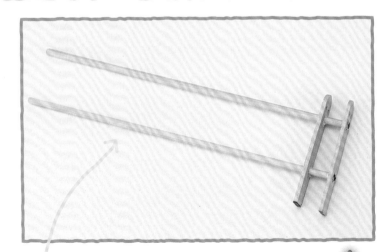

1 Hold together two lolly sticks so that they are lined up and drill holes with a craft drill as shown. Cut the lolly sticks down to 70mm with a craft knife.

2 Cut off two 200mm lengths of skewer. Thread them onto the lolly sticks so that the lolly sticks are one lolly-stick width apart.

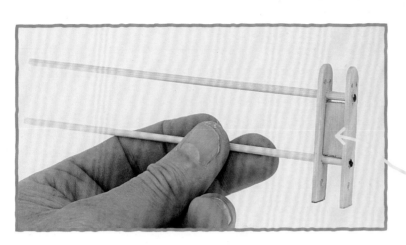

3 Cut off a short section of lolly stick and glue it into the gap with PVA glue. This will be the **ornithopter** body.

4 To make the wings, straighten then fold two paper clips with pliers to make the dogleg shape shown.

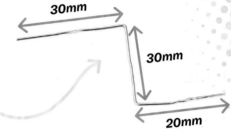

30mm

30mm

20mm

5 Cut two more 200mm skewers for the wing arms with a craft knife. Cut a notch in one end of each, and a groove to fit the centre of the wire.

6 Fit a paper clip wire in place on each skewer and wrap button thread round to secure it. Fix the thread with a knot and cover it all with PVA glue. Allow to dry.

7 Fit the wing wires into the small holes on the body. Thread a bead on each and bend the wires round to hold them on.

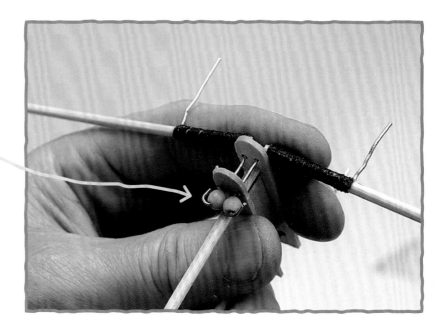

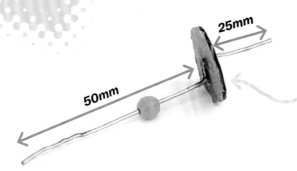

25mm

50mm

8 Make another dogleg from a paper clip as shown. Draw, cut out and glue on a 20mm circle of card to act as a washer, using super glue. Allow to dry.

9 Fit the wire on the body and make a hook at the end.

10 Straighten out another paper clip, make the hook as shown and wrap the rest around the back end of the upper skewer.

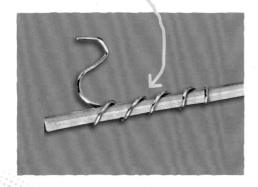

11 Cut out one side of a shopping bag with scissors. Lay the mechanism on the bag and draw round it to give the shape shown. Cut it out.

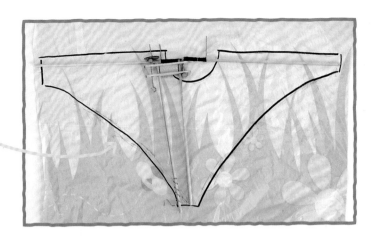

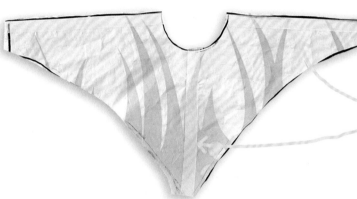

12 Apply two strips of double-sided tape to the top and one down the middle.

13 Peel off the tape backing to stick the plastic to the upper skewer on the body and wrap around the wing skewers.

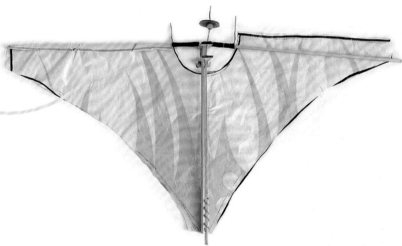

14 Cut a coffee stirring stick in half. Drill a 2mm hole in each end for the wires, roughly 40mm apart. Fit the coffee sticks on to the wires as shown. This will be the crank.

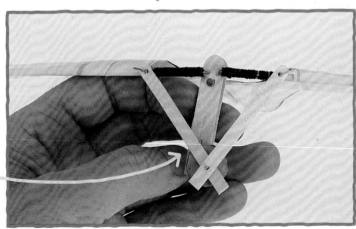

15 Bend the wing wires over to secure the coffee sticks. Cut off a small section of eraser and press it over the crank handle to secure it.

Make sure the crank can still move!

16 To make the tail, lay out three whole coffee sticks over plastic as shown. Draw round them. The plastic shape should be slightly larger all round, except at the top. Cut it out. Use double-sided tape to fix the two edges over the side sticks. Cut a 75mm piece of coffee stick for the crosspiece. Glue in place with PVA glue. When dry, trim to fit.

17 Unfold and wrap a paper clip round the end of the central stick as shown.

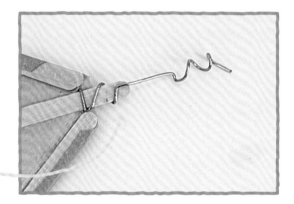

HOW IT WORKS

Ornithopters fly by mimicking the up-and-down flapping of a bird's wings. As the machine travels through the air, the wings push air downwards, producing lift. The flapping movement replaces the rotary movement of a propeller, or the thrust from a jet engine. Forward movement is provided by the elastic band releasing energy.

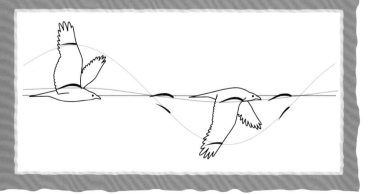

18 Wrap the other end of the tail paper clip round the end of the upper skewer on the body. Attach the elastic band between the two hooks on the lower skewer.

19 Wind up the model by turning the crank handle (wire on the eraser). Throw the ornithopter as you release the crank. Make adjustments to the tail for the best flight.

If it stalls in flight, lower the tail

Normal flight

If it dives in flight, raise the tail

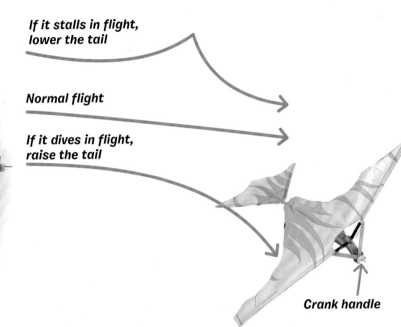

Crank handle

FLIP-FLAP!

REAL-WORLD ENGINEERING

Ornithopters date back around 800 years (even Leonardo Da Vinci invented one – see above). But the first successful manned ornithopter flight took place in 1942. This machine had a 3-horsepower motorcycle engine which meant it could take off from the ground. The designer, Adalbert Schmid, then cruised along for 15 minutes at about 60 km/h (37 mph).

AIR-POWERED ROCKET

This rocket is foot- rather than fuel-operated! Stand by... 3, 2, 1...

TOOLS:
- Craft drill
- Screwdriver
- PVA glue
- Small clamp
- Craft knife
- Ruler
- Gaffer tape

YOU WILL NEED:

15mm pipe insulation

15mm pipe

Craft foam

2 litre fizzy drink bottle

Craft cork

Two 15mm pipe clips with screws

300mm length of garden hose

Wood offcuts, about 500mm long

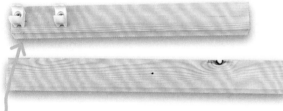

1 Screw the pipe clips onto one of the wood offcuts, close to the end as shown.

2 Glue the two offcuts together in a T shape with PVA glue. Hold them in place with a clamp as the glue dries. This will be the stand.

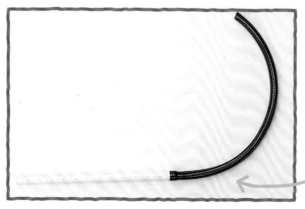

3 Cut off a 300mm length of 15mm pipe with a craft knife. Fit the hose on one end. Warming the end of the hose in a cup of hot water makes it easier to fit.

4 Cut a 250mm length of pipe insulation with a craft knife. Press a cork into the end. This is the rocket body.

5 Use a craft knife to cut three triangle fin shapes from craft foam, 100 x 35 x 105mm. Cut three 105mm slots in the rocket body and fit the fins in place.

6 Clamp the pipe to the stand as shown. Fit the bottle over the end of the hose and seal it with gaffer tape.

7 Fit the rocket over the pipe.

Stamp on the bottle to launch the rocket into orbit!

FFOOMM!

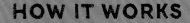

HOW IT WORKS

Stamping on the bottle forces air into the tube and blows the rocket model straight up. Once airborne, the fins keep it pointing forwards as it flies, like those on a real rocket. The weight of the cork pulls the front of the rocket round when it reaches the top of its flight and points it back down to Earth

GLOSSARY

GRAF ZEPPELIN LZ 127   7s

POSTES

REPUBLIQUE POPULAIRE
REVOLUTIONNAIRE DE GUINÉE

IMPRESSOR S.A. (SWITZERLAND) + P. GAUDARD

CROW'S FOOT KNOT

(above)

CROW'S FOOT HITCH KNOT

(below)

AIR RESISTANCE

(see Drag)

AIRSHIP

An aircraft that is lighter than air, also called an aerostat. It is essentially a bag full of a lighter-than-air gas, but unlike a balloon, has its own power. Early ones carried a crew, and the largest carried passengers. In time, helium replaced hydrogen – which is flammable – as the lifting gas. This was first done in the United States, where large amounts of helium were first discovered.

There are three main types of airship: non-rigid 'blimps'; semi-rigid, with a supporting structure; and rigid zeppelins. Airships were used less over time as aeroplane design developed, but they are still made for observation and research, advertising and tourism, for which their ability to hover for long periods is a big advantage.

DISPLACE

To push aside – as in, the amount of a fluid (gas or liquid) displaced by an object floating in it

DRAG

A kind of friction that opposes an object's direction of movement, and so slows it down. Drag is also known as air resistance, for objects moving in air, or fluid resistance, for objects moving in water.

GYROSOCOPE

A wheel mounted on a spindle within a metal frame. When spinning freely on a flat surface, it stays upright (resisting gravity) and can even maintain a sideways spin and balance on a string. Its ability to resist any change to its spinning direction makes it a vital navigation instrument on aeroplanes, helicopters and space probes, as it feeds back information on what a craft's position is, relative to where it should be.

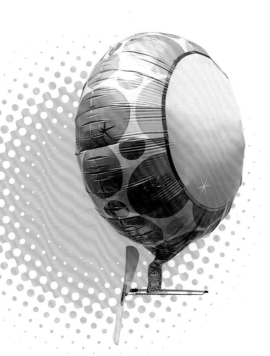

LIFT

The force that opposes the weight of an aircraft to keep it in the air. The flow of air has to be turned by all or some part of the aircraft, and it has to be moving to do this. In aeroplanes (and birds!), lift is mostly generated by the wings.

LOW DENSITY

A low concentration of mass in a substance. Density is a measure of how much mass there is in a certain volume of a substance. A low-density substance, such as sponge, has a large volume but low mass. Gases have a lower density than liquids or solids. While the density of a liquid or solid remains broadly constant, the density of a gas can vary widely, depending on its temperature and pressure.

ORNITHOPTER

An aircraft that flies by flapping its wings like a bird. These flying machines are usually built to the same scale as a bird. Among the many variations on the design was Lawrence Hargrave's idea for small wings that powered up larger wings. Percival Spencer and Jack Stephenson flew the first successful unmanned ornithopter in 1961. Called the Spencer Orniplane, it had a wingspan of 2.3 m (5ft 0.7in) and operated with a compact, two-stroke engine.

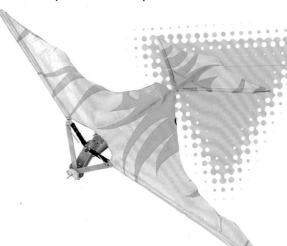

TERMINAL VELOCITY

The fastest speed reached by an object falling through a fluid, such as a skydiver freefalling through air to the ground

THERMAL

An upward current of warm air rising from the ground or a low-lying structure. Warm air near the surface of the ground expands and becomes lighter than the surrounding air so it rises, gradually cooling until it stops when its temperature is the same as the surrounding air. Urban areas and roads are good sources of thermals. Cumulus clouds often rest at the top of thermals, showing their presence. They may line up in rows called 'cloud streets' by glider pilots.

INDEX

THE AUTHOR

Rob Ives is a former maths and science teacher, now a designer and paper engineer living in Cumbria, UK. He creates science- and project-based children's books, including *Paper Models that Rock!* and *Paper Automata*. He specializes in character-based paper animations and all kinds of fun and fascinating science projects, and often visits schools to talk about design technology and demonstrate his models. Rob's other series for Hungry Tomato include *Tabletop Battles* and *Amazing Science Experiments*.

Picture Credits
(abbreviations: t = top; b = bottom; c = centre; l = left; r = right)

Shutterstock.com: 3Dsculptor 6tr & 29br; Boris15 30tl; Leo Blanchette 27br; Richard Thornton 9br & 31bl

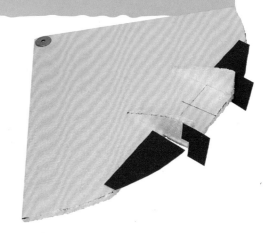